100

things you should know about

OCEANS

100

things you should know about

OCEANS

Clare Oliver

Consultant: Clive Carpenter

BARNES
&NOBLE
BOOKS
NEW YORK

First published in 2003 by
Miles Kelly Publishing Ltd
Bardfield Centre, Great Bardfield, Essex, CM7 4SL, U.K.

2 4 6 8 10 9 7 5 3 1

Publishing Director: Anne Marshall
Project Management: Belinda Gallagher
Assistant Editors: Nicola Jessop, Nicola Sail
Designer: John Christopher, White Design
Proofreader and Indexer: Lynn Bresler

Library of Congress Cataloging-in-Publication Data on
file at the Library of Congress

2004 Barnes & Noble Books

ISBN 0-7607-5967-7

Printed and bound in China

ACKNOWLEDGMENTS
The Publishers would like to thank the following artists who have
contributed to this book:

Kuo Kang Chen
Peter Dennis
Richard Draper
Nicholas Forder
Chris Forsey
Terry Gabbey
Studio Galante
Alan Harris

Kevin Maddison
Janos Marffy
Alan Male
Steve Roberts
Martin Sanders
Mike Saunders
Gwen Tourret
Rudi Vizi

Cartoons by Mark Davis at Mackerel

Contents

Water world

1 Oceans cover more than two thirds of the Earth's rocky surface. Their total area is about 140 million sq mi (362 million sq km), which means there is more than twice as much ocean as land! All the oceans flow into each other, but we know them as four different oceans—the Pacific, Atlantic, Indian, and Arctic. Our landmasses, the continents, rise out of the oceans.

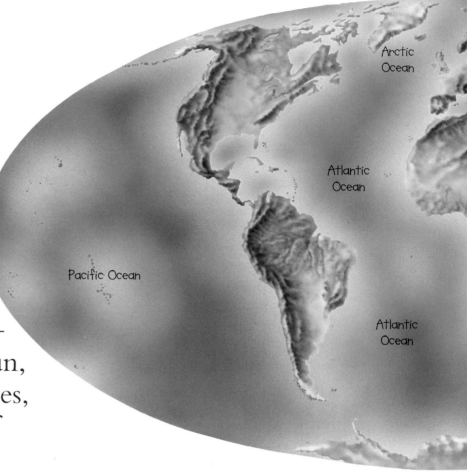

Arctic Ocean

Atlantic Ocean

Pacific Ocean

Atlantic Ocean

2 The largest, deepest ocean is the Pacific. It covers nearly half of our planet and is almost as big as the other three oceans put together! In places, the Pacific is so deep that the Earth's tallest mountain, Everest, would sink without a trace.

► Mount Everest is the highest point on Earth, rising to 29,078ft (8,863m). Parts of the Pacific Ocean are deeper than 30,000ft (10,000m).

The deepest parts of the Pacific would cover Mount Everest without trace

Indian Ocean

▲ The world's oceans cover most of our planet. Each ocean is made up of smaller bodies of water called seas.

Light hits the surface of the water

▶ A cup of sea water appears see-through. It is only when you look at a large area of sea that it has color.

Scattered blue and green

3 **Oceans can look blue, green, or gray.** This is because of the way light hits the surface. Water soaks up the red parts of light but scatters the blue-green parts, making the sea look different shades of blue or green.

4 **Seas can be red or dead.** A sea is a small part of an ocean. The Red Sea, for example, is the part of the Indian Ocean between Egypt and Saudi Arabia. Asia's Dead Sea isn't a true sea, but a landlocked lake. We call it a sea because it is a large body of water.

I DON'T BELIEVE IT!
97 percent of the world's water is in the oceans. Just a fraction is in freshwater lakes and rivers.

5 **There are streams in the oceans.** All the water in the oceans is constantly moving, but in some places it flows as currents, which take particular paths. One of these is the warm Gulf Stream, which travels around the edge of the Atlantic Ocean.

Ocean features

6 There are plains, mountains, and valleys under the oceans, in areas called basins. Each basin has a rim (the flat continental shelf that meets the shore) and sides (the continental slope that drops away from the shelf). In the ocean basin there are flat abyssal plains, steep hills, huge underwater volcanoes called seamounts, and deep valleys called trenches.

▼ Magma (molten rock) escapes from the seabed to form a ridge. This ridge has collapsed to form a rift valley.

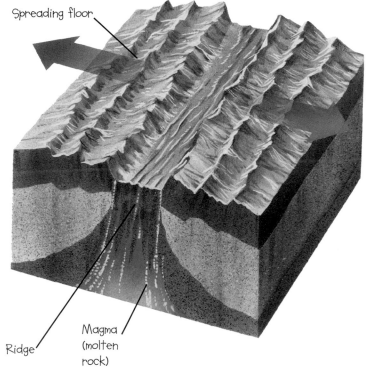

Spreading floor

Ridge

Magma (molten rock)

Land

Continental shelf

Continental slope

Spreading ridge

Abyssal trench

Abyssal hills

▲ Under the oceans there is a landscape similar to that found on land.

7 The ocean floor is spreading. Molten (liquid) rock inside the Earth seeps from holes on the seabed. As the rock cools, it forms new sections of floor that creep slowly out. Scientists have proved this fact by looking at layers of rock on the ocean floor. There are matching stripes of rock either side of a ridge. Each pair came from the same hot rock eruption, then slowly spread out.

Sea mount

Volcanic island

Ocean trench

▼ An atoll is a ring-shaped coral reef that encloses a deep lagoon. It can form when a volcanic island sinks underwater.

1. Coral starts to grow

4. Coral atoll is left behind

2. Lagoon appears around volcano

3. Volcano disappears

8 **Some islands are swallowed by the ocean.** Sometimes, a ring-shaped coral reef called an atoll marks where an island once was. The coral reef built up around the island. After the volcano blew its top, the reef remained.

▶ There are more Hawaiian islands still to come—Loihi is just visible beneath the water's surface.

9 **New islands are born all the time.** When an underwater volcano erupts, its lava cools in the water. Layers of lava build up, and the volcano grows in size. Eventually, it is tall enough to peep above the waves. The Hawaiian islands rose from the sea like this.

9

Tides and shores

10 **The sea level rises and falls twice each day along the coast.** This is known as high and low tides. Tides happen because of the pull of the Moon, which lifts water from the part of the Earth's surface facing it.

▼ At high tide, the sea rises up the shore and dumps seaweed, shells, and driftwood. Most coasts have two high tides and two low tides every day.

High tides happen at the same time each day on opposite sides of the Earth

At high tide the water level rises

At low tide the water level goes down again

11 **Spring tides are especially high.** They occur twice a month, when the Moon is in line with the Earth and the Sun. Then, the Sun's pulling force joins the Moon's and seawater is lifted higher than usual. The opposite happens when the Moon and Sun are at right angles to the Earth. Then, their pulling powers work against each other causing weak neap tides—the lowest high tides and low tides.

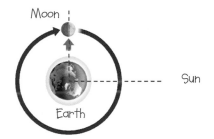
Moon
Sun
Earth

◄ Neap tides occur when the Sun and Moon are at right angles to each other and pulling in different directions.

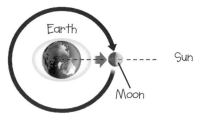
Earth
Sun
Moon

► Spring tides occur when the Sun and the Moon are lined up and pulling together.

12 The sea is strong enough to carve into rock. Pounding waves batter coastlines and erode, or wear away, the rock.

▼ Waves can create amazing shapes such as pillars called sea stacks.

Sea stack

Arch

▲ A tsunami can travel faster than a jumbo jet.

15 Tidal waves are the most powerful waves. Also known as tsunamis, they happen when underwater earthquakes trigger tremendous shock waves. These whip up a wall of water that travels across the sea's surface.

13 Sand is found on bars and spits, as well as beaches. It is made up of grains of worn-down rock and shell. Sand collects on shorelines and spits, but also forms on offshore beaches called sand bars. Spits are narrow ridges of worn sand and pebbles.

I DON'T BELIEVE IT!
The biggest tsunami was taller than five Statues of Liberty! It hit the Japanese Ryuku Islands in 1771.

14 Some shores are swampy. This makes the border between land and sea hard to pinpoint. Muddy coastlines include tropical mangrove swamps that are flooded by salty water from the sea.

▶ The stiltlike roots of mangrove trees take in both air and water.

Life in a rock pool

16 Rock pools are teeming with all kinds of creatures. Limpets are a kind of shellfish. They live on rocks and in pools at shorelines. Here, they eat slimy, green algae, but they have to withstand the crashing tide. They cling to the rock with their muscular foot, only moving when the tide is out.

17 Some anemones fight with harpoons. Beadlet anemones will sometimes fight over a feeding ground. Their weapon is the poison they usually use to stun their prey. They shoot tiny hooks like harpoons at each other until the weakest one gives in.

▲ Anemones are named after flowers, because of their petal-like arms.

18 Starfish can grow new arms. They may have as many as 40 arms, or rays. If a predator grabs hold of one, the starfish abandons the ray, and uses the others to make its getaway!

◄ Starfish are relatives of brittle stars, sea urchins, and sea cucumbers.

19 **Hermit crabs do not have shells.** Most crabs shed their shells as they outgrow them, but the hermit crab does not have a shell. It borrows the leftover shell of a dead whelk or other mollusk—whatever it can squeeze into to protect its soft body. These crabs have even been spotted using a coconut shell as a home!

▶ Hermit crabs protect their soft bodies in a borrowed shell.

FIND THE SHELL

Can you find the names of four shells in the puzzle below ?

1. alcm   2. lesmus
3. teroys 4. hewkl

1. Clam 2. Mussel
3. Oyster 4. Whelk

20 **Sea urchins wear a disguise.** Green sea urchins sometimes drape themselves with bits of shell, pebble, and seaweed. This makes the urchin more difficult for predators, or hunters, to spot.

◀ There are about 4,500 different types of sponge in the sea.

21 **Sponges are animals!** They are very simple creatures that filter food from sea water. The natural sponge that you might use in the bath is a long-dead, dried-out sponge.

13

Colorful coral

22 **Tiny animals build huge underwater walls.** These are built up from coral, the leftover skeletons of sea creatures called polyps. Over millions of years, enough skeletons pile up to form huge, wall-like structures called reefs. Coral reefs are full of hiding places and make brilliant habitats for all sorts of amazing, colorful sea life.

23 **The world's biggest shellfish lives on coral reefs.** Giant clams grow to well over 3ft (90cm)— big enough for you to bathe in its shell!

24 **Seahorse dads have the babies.** They don't exactly give birth, but they store the eggs in a pouch on their belly. When the eggs are ready to hatch, a stream of miniature seahorses billows out from the dad's pouch.

▶ Baby seahorses stream out of their father's pouch and into the sea.

Parrot fish

Giant clam

Clownfish

25

Some fish go to the cleaners. Cleaner wrasse are little fish that are paid for cleaning! Larger fish, such as groupers and moray eels, visit the wrasse. The wrasse nibble all the parasites and other bits of dirt off the bigger fishes' bodies—what a feast!

26

Clownfish are sting-proof. Most creatures steer clear of an anemone's stinging tentacles. But the clownfish swims among the stingers, where it's safe from predators. Strangely, the anemone doesn't seem to sting the clownfish.

I DON'T BELIEVE IT!
You can see the Great Barrier Reef from space! At 1,200mi (2,000km) long, it is the largest structure ever built by living creatures.

27

Some fish look like stones. Stone fish rest on the seabed, looking just like the rocks that surround them. If they are spotted, the poisonous spines on their backs can stun an attacker in seconds.

Lion fish

Cleaner wrasse fish

Stone fish

▲ Tropical coral reefs are the habitat of an amazing range of marine plants and creatures.

Swimming machines

28 There are more than 21,000 different types of fish in the sea. They range from huge whale sharks to tiny gobies. Almost all are covered in scales and use fins and a muscular tail to power through the water. Like their freshwater cousins, sea fish have slits called gills that take oxygen from the water so they can breathe.

29 The oarfish is bigger than an oar—it is as long as four canoes! It is the longest bony fish and is found in all the world's oceans. Oarfish are handsome creatures—they have a striking red fin along the length of their back.

◄ People once thought oarfish swam horizontally through the water. Now they know they swim upright.

▶ At about 10ft (3m) long, sunfish are the biggest bony fish in the oceans. They feed on plankton.

30 Sunfish like sunbathing! Ocean sunfish are very large, broad fish that can weigh as much as a ton. They are named after their habit of sunbathing on the surface of the open ocean.

▶ Flying fish feed near the surface so they are easy to find. Their gliding flight helps them escape most hunters.

32 Flying fish cannot really fly. Fish can't survive out of water, but flying fish sometimes leap above the waves when they are traveling at high speeds. They use their winglike fins to keep them in the air for as long as 30 seconds.

▲ In a large group called a school, fish like these yellow snappers have less chance of being picked off by a predator.

31 Not all fish are the same shape. Cod or mackerel are what we think of as a normal fish shape, but fish come in all shapes and sizes. Flounder and other flatfish have squashed-flat bodies. Eels are so long and thin that the biggest types look like snakes, while tiny garden eels resemble worms! And of course, seahorses and seadragons look nothing like other fish at all!

▶ The flounder's flattened shape and dull coloring help to camouflage (hide) it on the seabed.

QUIZ
1. Which fish like to sunbathe?
2. How many types of fish live in the sea?
3. How does a fish breathe?
4. Can flying fish really fly?

1. Sunfish 2. 21,000 3. With its gills 4. No

Shark!

33 Great whites are the scariest sharks in the oceans. These powerful predators have been known to kill people and can speed through the water at 20mph (30km/h). Unlike most fish, the great white is warm-blooded. This allows its muscles to work well, but also means the shark has to feed on plenty of meat.

▼ Basking sharks eat enormous amounts of plankton. They sieve through around 1,000 tons of water every hour.

▲ Great white sharks are fierce hunters. They will attack and eat almost anything, but prefer to feed on seals.

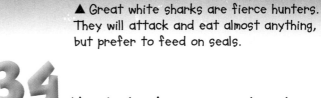

34 Most sharks are meat eaters. Herring are a favorite food for sand tiger and thresher sharks, while a hungry tiger shark will gobble up just about anything! Strangely, some of the biggest sharks take the smallest prey. Whale sharks and basking sharks eat tiny sea creatures called plankton.

SHARK PARTS

Study the labels to learn the shark's special features. Trace the shark without the labels, then see how many parts you can name.

► Hammerheads prey on other sharks and rays, bony fish, crabs and lobsters, octopus, and squid.

Dorsal fin

Ampullae of Lorenzini (to sense electricity from nearby fish)

Nostril

Jaw

Pectoral fin

Gill

Tail fin

Anal fin

Pelvic fin

36 Hammerhead sharks have a hammer–shaped head! With a nostril and an eye on each end of the "hammer," they swing their head from side to side. This gives them double the chance to see and sniff out any signs of a tasty catch.

35 Tiger sharks may have as many as 40 pups! The baby sharks develop in eggcases inside their mother's body. Many other sharks also reproduce like this, but it is not the only way. Hammerhead and gray reef shark babies develop inside their mother, not in eggcases. Other sharks, such as dogfish and zebra sharks, lay eggcases straight into the sea, leaving the babies to fend for themselves.

▼ Tiger sharks leave their newborn pups to fend for themselves.

Whales and dolphins

37 **The biggest animal on the planet lives in the oceans.** It is the blue whale, measuring about 90ft (28m) in length and weighing up to 200 tons. It feeds by filtering tiny, shrimplike creatures called krill from the water—about 4 tons of krill a day! Like other great whales, it has special, sievelike parts in its mouth called baleen plates.

▲ As the sperm whale surfaces, it pushes out stale air through its blowhole. It fills its lungs with fresh air and dives down again.

38 **Whales and dolphins have to come to the surface for air.** This is because they are mammals, like humans. Sperm whales hold their breath the longest. They have been known to stay underwater for nearly two hours.

▲ Blue whale calves feed on their mother's rich milk until they are around eight months old.

41 **Killer whales play with their food.** They especially like to catch baby seals, which they toss into the air before eating. Killer whales are not true whales, but the largest dolphins. They have teeth for chewing, instead of baleen plates.

▲ Killer whales carry the baby seals out to sea before eating them.

▶ The beluga is a type of white whale. It makes a range of noises—whistles, clangs, chirps, and moos!

39 **Dolphins and whales sing songs to communicate.** The noisiest is the humpback whale, whose wailing noises can be heard for hundreds of miles. The sweetest is the beluga—nicknamed the "sea canary." Songs are used to attract a mate, or just to keep track of each other.

42 **Moby Dick was a famous white whale.** It starred in a book by Herman Melville about a white sperm whale and a whaler named Captain Ahab.

40 **The narwhal has a horn like a unicorn's.** This Arctic whale has a long, twirly tooth that spirals out of its head. The males use their tusks as a weapon when they are fighting over females.

▲ The narwhal's 10ft (3m) tusk seems too long for its body.

I DON'T BELIEVE IT!
Barnacles are shellfish. They attach themselves to ships' hulls, or the bodies of gray whales and other large sea animals.

Sleek swimmers

43 **Whales and dolphins are not the only sea mammals.** Seals, sea lions, and walruses are warm-blooded mammals that have adapted to ocean life. These creatures are known as pinnipeds, meaning "fin feet." They have flippers instead of legs—far more useful for swimming! They also have streamlined bodies and a layer of fatty blubber under the skin, to keep them warm in chilly waters.

▶ Most seals live in cold waters. Crabeater, leopard, and Weddell seals live in Antarctica. The northern seals, which live around the Arctic, include harp and bearded seals.

44 **Elephant seals are well named —they are truly enormous!** Southern elephant seal males can weigh over three and a half tons, while their northern cousins weigh at least two. During their three-month-long breeding season, males stay ashore to fight off any rivals. Unable to hunt for fish, some lose as much as half their body weight.

46 **Sea otters anchor themselves when they sleep.** These playful creatures live off the Pacific coast among huge forests of giant seaweed called kelp. When they take a snooze, they wrap a strand of kelp around their body to stop them being washed out to sea.

▲ Anchored to the kelp, a sea otter is free to crack open a crab shell—and snack!

45 **Walruses seem to change color!** When a walrus is in the water, it appears pale brown or even white. This is because blood drains from the skin's surface to stop the body losing heat. On land, the blood returns to the skin and walruses can look reddish brown or pink!

▼ Walruses use their tusks as weapons. They are also used to break breathing holes in the ice, and to help the walrus pull itself out of the water.

I DON'T BELIEVE IT!
Leopard seals sing in their sleep! These seals, found in the Antarctic, chirp and whistle while they snooze.

Ocean reptiles

47 Marine iguanas are the most seaworthy lizards. Most lizards prefer life on land, where it is easier to warm up their cold-blooded bodies, but marine iguanas depend on the sea for their food. They dive underwater to graze on the algae and seaweed growing on rocks.

▲ Marine iguanas are found around the Galapagos Islands in the Pacific. When they are not diving for food, they bask on the rocks that dot the island coastlines. The lizards' dark skin helps to absorb the Sun's heat.

48 Turtles come ashore only to lay their eggs. Although they are born on land, turtles head for the sea the minute they hatch. Females return to the beach where they were born to dig their nest. After they have laid their eggs, they go straight back to the water. Hawksbill turtles may lay up to 140 eggs in a clutch, while some green turtle females clock up 800 eggs in a year!

▲ In a single breeding season, a female green turtle may lay as many as ten clutches, each containing up to 80 eggs!

49

There are venomous (poisonous) snakes in the sea. Most stay close to land and come ashore to lay their eggs. Banded sea snakes, for example, cruise around coral reefs in search of their favorite food, eels. But the yellow-bellied sea snake never leaves the water. It gives birth to live babies in the open ocean.

▼ Banded sea snakes use venom (poison) to stun prey, but the yellow-bellied sea snake has a sneakier trick. Once its colorful underside has attracted some fish, it darts back—so the fish are next to its open mouth! The venom of sea snakes is more powerful than that of any land snake.

Yellow-bellied sea snake

Banded sea snake

MIX AND MATCH

Can you match these sea turtles to their names?

1. Green 2. Hawksbill
3. Leatherback 4. Loggerhead

1c 2b 3d 4a

a.

b.

c.

d.

▼ Leatherbacks are the biggest turtles in the world and can grow to 13ft (4m) in length.

50

Leatherbacks dive up to 4,000ft (1,220m) for dinner. These turtles hold the record for being the biggest sea turtles and for making the deepest dives. Leatherbacks feed mostly on jellyfish but their diet also includes mollusks, crabs, starfish, and sea urchins.

Icy depths

51 Few creatures can survive in the dark, icy-cold ocean depths. Food is so hard to come by, the deep-sea anglerfish does not waste energy chasing prey—it has developed a clever fishing trick. A stringy "fishing rod" with a glowing tip extends from its dorsal fin or hangs above its jaw. This attracts smaller fish to the anglerfish's big mouth.

▼ Anglerfish are black or brown for camouflage. Only their glowing "fishing rod" is visible in the gloom.

▼ The light created by deep-sea fish, or by bacteria living on their bodies, is known as biological light, or bioluminescence.

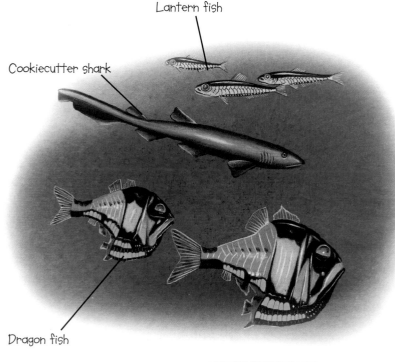

Lantern fish

Cookiecutter shark

Dragon fish

52 Some deep-sea fish glow in the dark. As well as tempting prey, light also confuses predators. About 1,500 different deep-sea fish give off light. The lantern fish's whole body glows, while the dragon fish has light organs dotted along its sides and belly. Just the belly of the cookiecutter shark gives off a ghostly glow. Cookiecutters take cookie-shaped bites out of their prey's body!

53 **Black swallowers have huge appetites!** These strange fish are just 10in (25cm) long but can eat fish far bigger than themselves. Their loose jaws unhinge to fit over the prey. Then the stretchy body expands to take in their enormous meal.

▼ Like many deep-sea fish, black swallowers have smooth, scaleless skin.

▲ The viperfish is named for its long, snakelike fangs.

54 **Viperfish have teeth that are invisible in the dark.** They swim around with their jaws wide open. Deep-sea shrimp often see nothing until they are right inside the viperfish's mouth.

► Tubeworms grow around deep-sea volcanoes called black smokers.

I DON'T BELIEVE IT!
Female deep-sea anglerfish grow to 4ft (120cm) in length, but the males are a tiny 2in (6cm)!

55 **On the seabed, there are worms as long as cars!** These are giant tubeworms and they cluster around hot spots on the ocean floor. They feed on tiny particles that they filter from the water.

Amazing journeys

56 Many ocean animals travel incredible distances. Spiny lobsters spend the summer feeding off the coast of Florida, but head south in autumn to deeper waters. They travel about 30mi (50km) along the seabed, in columns that may be more than 50-strong. They keep together by touch, using their long, spiky antennae (feelers).

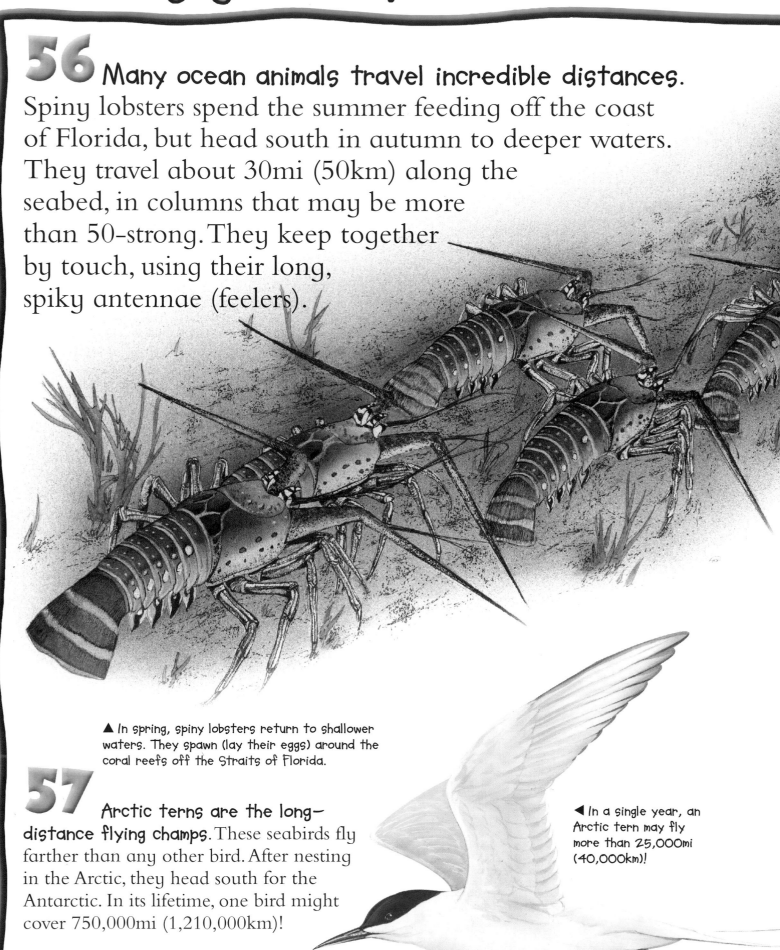

▲ In spring, spiny lobsters return to shallower waters. They spawn (lay their eggs) around the coral reefs off the Straits of Florida.

57 Arctic terns are the long—distance flying champs. These seabirds fly farther than any other bird. After nesting in the Arctic, they head south for the Antarctic. In its lifetime, one bird might cover 750,000mi (1,210,000km)!

◄ In a single year, an Arctic tern may fly more than 25,000mi (40,000km)!

58 Gray whales migrate, or travel, farther than any other mammal. There are two main gray whale populations in the Pacific. One spends summer off the Alaskan coast. In winter they migrate south to Mexico to breed. The whales may swim nearly 12,000mi (20,000km) in a year. The other gray whale group spends summer off the coast of Russia, then travels south to Korea.

▶ Gray whales spend summer in the Bering Sea, feeding on tiny, shrimplike creatures called amphipods. They spend their breeding season, December to March, in the warmer waters off Mexico.

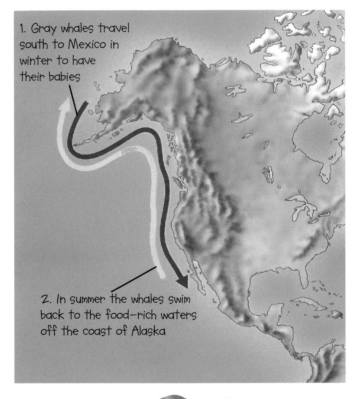

1. Gray whales travel south to Mexico in winter to have their babies

2. In summer the whales swim back to the food-rich waters off the coast of Alaska

59 Baby loggerhead turtles make a two-year journey. They are born on beaches in Japan. The hatchlings soon set off across the Pacific to Mexico, a journey of 6,000mi (10,000km). They spend about five years there before returning to Japan to breed.

▼ Not all loggerhead hatchlings make it to the sea. As they race down the beach, some are picked off by hungry gulls or crabs.

I DON'T BELIEVE IT!
Eels and salmon swim thousands of miles from the sea to spawn in the same river nurseries where they were born.

On the wing

60 **Wandering albatrosses are the biggest seabirds.** An albatross has a wingspan of around 10ft (3m)—about the length of two bicycles! These seabirds are so large, they take off by launching from a cliff. Albatrosses spend months at sea. They are such expert gliders that they even sleep on the wing. To feed, they land on the sea, where they sit and catch creatures such as squid.

61 **Gannets wear airbag shock absorbers.** The gannet's feeding technique is to plummet headfirst into the ocean and catch a fish in its beak. It dives at high-speed and hits the water hard. Luckily, the gannet's head is protected with sacs of air that absorb most of the shock.

► A gannet dives and captures a fishy meal in its beak.

62 **Puffins nest in burrows.** While many birds jostle for space on a high cliff ledge, puffins dig a burrow on the clifftop. Here, they lay a single egg. Both parents feed the chick for the first six weeks.

▼ Puffins often scrape their own burrows, or they may take over an abandoned rabbit hole.

SEE THE SEABIRD!
See if you can match these seabirds to their correct names.
1. Cormorant 2. Gray headed gull
3. Black tern

a.   b.   c.

1c 2b 3a

64 **Boobies dance to attract a mate.** There are two types of booby, blue or red-footed. The dancing draws attention to the male's colorful feet. Perhaps this stops the females from mating with the wrong type of bird.

▼ Boobies are tropical seabirds that nest in colonies.

63 **Frigate birds puff up a balloon for their mate.** Male frigate birds have a bright-red pouch on their throat. They inflate, or blow up, the pouch as part of their display to attract a female.

▲ A frigate bird shows off to its mate.

Perfect penguins

65 Macaroni, chinstrap, jackass, and emperor are all types of penguin. There are 17 different types in total, and most live around the Antarctic. Penguins feed on fish, squid, and krill. Their black-and-white plumage is important camouflage. Seen from above, a penguin's black back blends in with the water. The white belly is hard to distinguish from the sunlit surface of the sea.

Chinstrap penguin

66 Penguins can swim, but not fly. They have oily, waterproofed feathers and flipper-like wings. Instead of lightweight, hollow bones—like a flying bird's—some penguins have solid, heavy bones. This enables them to stay underwater longer when diving for food. Emperor penguins can stay under for 15 minutes or more.

I DON'T BELIEVE IT!
The fastest swimming bird is the gentoo penguin. It has been known to swim at speeds of 16mph (27km/h)!

▶ Penguins have a layer of fat under their feathers to protect them in the icy water.

Gentoo penguin

Adélie penguin

King penguin

Emperor penguin

67 **Emperor penguin dads balance an egg on their feet.** They do this to keep their egg off the Antarctic ice, where it would freeze. The female leaves her mate with the egg for the whole two months that it takes to hatch. The male has to go without food during this time. When the chick hatches, the mother returns and both parents help to raise it.

▶ A downy emperor penguin chick cannot find its own food in the sea. It must wait until it has grown its waterproof, adult plumage.

▲ An Adélie penguin builds its nest from stones and small rocks.

68 **Some penguins build stone circles.** This is the way that Adélie and gentoo penguins build nests on the shingled shores where they breed. First, they scrape out a small dip with their flippered feet and then they surround the hollow with a circle of pebbles.

Harvests from the sea

◀ Fishermen attach buoys to their lobster traps, so they can remember where to find them again.

69 **Oysters come from beds—and lobsters from traps!** The animals in the oceans feed other sea creatures, and they feed us, too! To gather oysters, fishermen raise them on trays or poles in the water. First, they collect oyster larvae, or babies. They attract them by putting out sticks hung with shells. Lobster larvae are too difficult to collect, but the adults are caught in traps filled with fish bait.

70 **Some farmers grow seaweed.** Seaweed is delicious to eat, and is also a useful ingredient in products such as ice cream and plant fertilizer. In shallow, tropical waters, people grow their own on plots of seabed.

▲ The harvested seaweed can be dried in the sun to preserve it.

▶ The oil platform's welded-steel legs rest on the seabed. They support the platform around 50ft (15m) above the surface of the water.

Derrick

Crane

Helicopter landing pad

Flare

Oil-processing area

71 **Sea minerals are big business.** Minerals are useful substances that we mine from the ground—and oceans are full of them! The most valuable are oil and gas, which are pumped from the seabed and piped ashore or transported in huge supertankers. Salt is another important mineral. In hot, low-lying areas, people build walls to hold shallow pools of sea water. The water dries up in the sun, leaving behind crystals of salt.

72 **There are gemstones under the sea.** Pearls are made by oysters. If a grain of sand is lodged inside an oyster's shell, it irritates its soft body. The oyster coats the sand with a substance called nacre, which is also used to line the inside of the shell. Over the years, more nacre builds up and the pearl gets bigger.

QUIZ
1. What are the young of lobster called?
2. What substances are pumped from the seabed?
3. Is seaweed edible?
4. Which gemstone is made by oysters?

1. Larvae 2. Oil and gas
3. Yes 4. Pearl

▶ Pearl divers carry an oyster knife for prising open the oyster's shell.

First voyages

73 **The first boats were made from tree trunks.** Early people hollowed out tree trunks to craft their own dugouts. For several hundred years, the Maori peoples of New Zealand made log war canoes, decorating them with beautiful carvings.

▶ Viking longboats were clinker-built, which means that they were made of overlapping planks of wood.

▼ Maori war canoes were usually carved out of kauri pine trunks.

▶ A painted eye on the trireme's hull was believed to protect the boat from evil spirits.

74 **Greek warships were oar-some!** The ancient Greeks used people-power and sails to move their ships through the water. Triremes were warships rowed by three layers of oarsmen. In battle, the trireme was steered straight at an enemy ship like a battering ram.

77 Boats found the way to a new world.

The 1400s were an amazing time of exploration and discovery. One explorer, Christopher Columbus, set sail from Spain in 1492 with a fleet of three ships. He hoped to find a new trade route to India, but instead he found the Americas! Before then, they were not even on the map!

▶ Columbus's fleet consisted of the *Niña,* the *Pinta,* and the *Santa Maria.*

75 Dragons guarded Viking longboats.

Scandinavian seafarers decorated their boats' prows with carvings of dragons and serpents to terrify their enemies. Built from overlapping planks, Viking longboats were very seaworthy. Leif Ericson was the first Viking to cross the Atlantic Ocean to Newfoundland, in North America just over 1,000 years ago.

76 It is thought that Chinese navigators made the first compass—like device about 2,500 years ago.

Compasses use the Earth's magnetism to show the directions of north, south, east and west. They are used at sea, where there are no landmarks. The navigators used lodestone, a naturally magnetic rock, to magnetize the needle.

▶ Early compasses were very simple. During the 1300s compasses became more detailed.

BOAT SCRAMBLE!
Unscramble the letters to find the names of six different types of boat.
1. leacvar 2. chenroos
3. rarlewt 4. coclear
5. leglay 6. pecpril

1. Caravel 2. Schooner
3. Trawler 4. Coracle
5. Galley 6. Clipper

Pirates!

78 **Pirates once ruled the high seas.** Pirates are sailors who attack and board other ships to steal their cargoes. Their golden age was during the 1600s and 1700s. This was when heavily laden ships carried treasures, weapons, and goods back to Europe from colonies in the Americas, Africa, and Asia. Edward Teach, better known as Blackbeard, was one of the most terrifying pirates. He attacked ships off the coast of North America during the early 1700s. To frighten his victims, it is said that he used to set fire to his own beard!

79 **There were women pirates, too.** Piracy was a man's world, but some women also took to the high seas. Mary Read and Anne Bonny were part of a pirate crew sailing around the Caribbean. They wore men's clothes and used fighting weapons, including daggers, cutlasses, and pistols.

▼ Pirate weapons had often been stolen on previous raids. The men fought to the death.

80 **There are still pirates on the oceans.** Despite police patrols who watch for pirates and smugglers, a few pirates still operate. Luxury yachts are an easy target and in the South China Sea, pirate gangs on motor boats even attack large merchant ships.

▼ Divers have found some extraordinary hoards of treasure on board sunken galleons.

81 **There is treasure lying under the sea.** Over the centuries, many ships sank in storms or hit reefs. They include pirate ships loaded with stolen booty. Some ships were deliberately sunk by pirates. The bed of the Caribbean Sea is littered with the remains of Spanish galleons, many of which still hold treasure!

PIRATE FLAG!

You will need:

paper   paints   brushes

The skull-and-crossbones is the most famous pirate flag, but it was not the only one. Copy one of these designs!

Going under

82 **A submarine has dived deeper than 33,000ft (10,000m).** The two-person *Trieste* made history in 1960 in an expedition to the Mariana Trench in the Pacific, the deepest part of any ocean. It took the submarine five hours to reach the bottom, a distance of 35,788ft (10,911m). On the way down, the extreme water pressure cracked part of the craft, but luckily, the two men inside returned to the surface unharmed.

▲ *Trieste* spent 20 minutes at the bottom of the Mariana Trench. The trench is so deep, you could stack the world's tallest building, the CN Tower, inside it 19 times (left)!

Mast to renew and expel air

Propeller

Mine

▶ The Americans used *Turtle* against the British in the War of Independence.

Propeller

83 **The first combat submarine was shaped like an egg!** *Turtle* was a one-person submarine that made its test dive in 1776. It was the first real submarine. It did not have an engine—it was driven by a propeller that was turned by hand! *Turtle* was built for war. It traveled just below the surface and could fix bombs to the bottom of enemy ships.

84

Divers have a spare pair of lungs. Scuba divers wear special breathing apparatus called "aqualungs." French divers Jacques Cousteau and Emile Gagnan came up with the idea of a portable oxygen supply. This meant that divers were able to swim freely for the first time, rather than wearing a heavy suit and helmet.

I DON'T BELIEVE IT!
In 1963 Jacques Cousteau built a village on the bed of the Red Sea. Along with four other divers, he lived there for a whole month.

◀ Divers control their breathing to make their oxygen supply last as long as possible.

85

The biggest submarines weighed 28,700 tons. They were Russian submarines called *Typhoons*, built in the 1970s and 1980s. As well as being the biggest subs, they were also the fastest, able to top 40 knots.

Periscope

Rudder

Living quarters

Torpedo firing tube

Engine room

▲ The *Typhoons* did not need to come up to refuel because they were nuclear-powered.

Diving plane

Superboats

86 **Some ships are invisible.** Stealth warships are not really invisible, of course, but they are hard to detect using radar. There are already materials being used for ships that can absorb some radar signals. Some paints can soak up radar, too, and signals are also bounced off in confusing directions by the ships' strange, angled hulls.

I DON'T BELIEVE IT!
People said *Titanic* was unsinkable. But it hit an iceberg and sank on its maiden voyage. More than 1,500 people drowned.

87 **The world's biggest ship is 1,502ft (458m) long.** It is a supertanker called *Jahre Viking*. Supertankers carry cargoes of oil around the world. They move slowly because they are so huge and heavy.

▲ An angled, sloping hull gives very little radar echo. This makes the stealth ship's location hard to pinpoint.

▼ The giant supertanker *Jahre Viking* is 226ft (74m) wide.

88
Not all boats ride the waves. Hovercrafts sit slightly above the water. They have a rubbery skirt that traps a cushion of air for them to ride on. Without the drag of the water to work against, hovercraft can cross the water much faster.

◄ Hovercraft can travel at up to 65 knots, or 72mph (120km/h).

▼ *Freedom Ship* will be over 4,000ft (1,300m) long. Aircraft "taxis" will be able to take off and land on its rooftop runway.

89
Ships can give piggybacks! Heavy-lift ships can sink part of their deck underwater, so a smaller ship can sail aboard for a free ride. Some ships carry planes. Aircraft carriers transport planes that are too small to carry enough fuel for long distances. The deck doubles up as a runway, where the planes take off and land.

90
Freedom Ship will resemble a floating city. It will be one of the first ocean cities, with apartments, shopping centers, a school, and a hospital. The people who live on *Freedom* will circle the Earth once every two years. By following the Sun, they will live in constant summertime!

43

Riding the waves

91 **The first sea sport was surfing.** It took off in the 1950s, but was invented centuries earlier in Hawaii. Hawaii is still one of the best places to surf —at Waimea Bay, surfers catch waves that are up to 35ft (11m) high. The record for the longest rides, though, are made off the coast of Mexico, where it is possible to surf for a mile or even more.

▶ Modern surfboards are made of super–light materials. This means they create little drag in the water—and the surfer can reach high speeds!

92 **A single boat towed 100 waterskiers!** This record was made off the coast of Australia in 1986 and no one has beaten it yet. The drag boat was a cruiser called *Reef Cat.*

◀ Waterskiing is now one of the most popular of all water sports.

QUIZ
1. What was the name of the fastest hydroplane?
2. When did jetskis go on sale?
3. Where is Waimea Bay?
4. What is a trimaran?

1. *Spirit of Australia*
2. 1973 3. Hawaii
4. A three-hulled boat

44

93 Jetskiers can travel at nearly 60mph (100km/h). Jetskis were developed in the 1960s. Their inventor was an American named Clayton Jacobsen who wanted to combine his two favorite hobbies—motorbikes and waterskiing. Today, some jetskiers are professional sportspeople.

◄ Jetskis first went on sale in 1973.

◄ Trimarans have three hulls, while catamarans have two.

94 Three hulls are sometimes better than one. Powerboating is an exciting, dangerous sport. Competitors are always trying out new boat designs that will race even faster. Multihulled boats minimize drag, but keep the boat steady. Trimarans have three slender, streamlined hulls that cut through the water.

95 Hydroplanes fly over the waves. They are a cross between a boat and a plane. Special "wings" raise the hull 6ft (1.8m) above the water. The fastest hydroplane ever was *Spirit of Australia*. Driven by Kenneth Warby, it sped along at more than 300mph (500km/h) over the water!

► Hydroplanes are motorboats that skim across the surface of the water.

Ocean stories

▼ Jason and the Argonauts steer their ship between two huge moving cliffs called the Cyanean Rocks. They faced many dangers on their journey.

96 The Greek hero Jason made an epic sea voyage. The ancient Greeks made up lots of sea adventure stories, probably because they lived on scattered islands. In the legend of the Argonauts, a hero called Jason sets off in a boat called the *Argo* with a band of brave men. He goes on a quest to find the Golden Fleece, a precious sheepskin guarded by a fierce dragon.

97 Neptune (or Poseidon) was an undersea god. Poseidon was the name used by the ancient Greeks and Neptune by the ancient Romans. Both civilizations pictured their god with a fork called a trident. They blamed their gods for the terrible storms that wrecked boats in the Mediterranean.

► Neptune raises his trident and whips up a storm.

▲ The beautiful goddess Aphrodite emerges from the sea.

99

Long ago, people believed in a giant sea monster, called the kraken. The stories were used to explain the dangers of the sea. Sightings of the giant squid might have inspired these tales.

▶ Mistaken for a monster! The 50ft (15m) long giant squid has eyes as big as dinner plates.

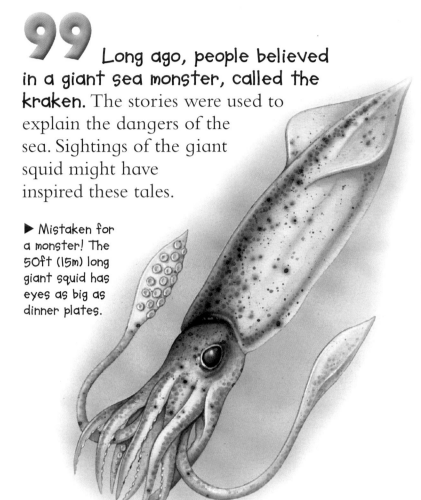

98

The Greek goddess of love was born in the sea. Aphrodite, said to be the daughter of Zeus, was born out of the foam of the sea. The Romans based their love goddess, Venus, on the same story. Lots of artists have painted her rising from the waves in a giant seashell.

100

Mermaids lured sailors to their deaths on the rocks. Mythical mermaids were said to be half-woman, half-fish. Folklore tells how the mermaids confused sailors with their beautiful singing—with the result that their ships were wrecked on the rocks.

▼ Mermaids were said to have a fishy tail instead of legs.

I DON'T BELIEVE IT!
A mermaid's purse is the name given to the eggcases of the dog shark. They look a little bit like handbags!

Index